15 3-

Spirit of the Nursery

Spirit of the Nursery

Jane Alexander

WATSON-GUPTILL PUBLICATIONS/NEW YORK

For James Alexander Tierney-Jones—

with a big hug and a kiss

First published in the United States in 2002 by
Watson-Guptill Publications
a division of VNU Business Media, Inc.
770 Broadway, New York, New York 10003
www.watsonguptill.com

First published in the UK in 2002 by Element
An imprint of HarperCollins*Publishers*
77-85 Fulham Palace Road
Hammersmith, London W6 8JB

1 2 3 4 5 6 / 07 06 05 04 03 02

Jane Alexander asserts the moral right
to be identified as the author of this work
Editor: Jillian Stewart
Design: Wheelhouse Creative
Production: Melanie Vandevelde

Library of Congress Control Number: 2001119258

ISBN: 0 8230 4902 7

Printed and bound in Hong Kong

Contents

Introduction

Why a nursery? A baby spends the first nine months of its life in the perfect environment, safe, protected, warm, secure. Soothed by the heartbeat of its mother, cushioned among soft layers of tissue—the womb is the safest place in the world to be. Then he or she is born, into a environment which is harsh, dangerous, and often frightening. It's no wonder that every parent wants to create a safe, secure environment for his or her newborn baby or young child. This is why high on almost every prospective parent's "to-do" list is the planning and decoration of the nursery.

Why do we do it? In actual fact a newborn baby doesn't really need a special room and certainly won't grumble if you have chosen Peter Rabbit when she'd rather have been surrounded by Winnie the Pooh. Let's be honest—we furnish nurseries first and foremost for ourselves. A very young baby probably won't even spend that much time in this lovingly prepared cocoon. A nursery, however, is a room of hope, of dreams, of nurturing and inspiration. It gives us the chance to replay our own childhood, to nurture the child within and allow its imagination free rein. A nursery is a small world of its own—a retreat from the sophisticated tastes and breakneck speed of the outside world. It is a timeless fantasy realm of slumber and lullabies, of fairy tales and nursery rhymes. Planning and decorating the nursery is also a profound psychological statement. "It's a rite of passage," says psychologist Sarah Dening, "it's a symbol that you are changing your house (and yourself) to accommodate a new person. It gives the child-to-come status."

So indulge yourself. Allow your imagination free rein. Let your inner child loose to play with a nursery. Allow all your hopes and dreams and wishes for your child to suffuse this special place. Just as in the fairy tales, when charms and spells were muttered over newborn babies, you can weave your own protective magic as you prepare this new cocoon. For this reason we'll be looking not just at the physical decoration and adornments of a nursery (which is, of course, vitally important), but at its energetic and spiritual reality too.

A baby is psychically very delicate and needs a soothing sanctuary. All too often we focus purely on a baby's physical needs and ignore its spiritual well-being. Hopefully this little book will give you food for thought and help you make your baby's nursery a place of warm, loving, peaceful energy.

Spirit of Space

Where should your baby sleep? It need not be an entire room. In fact, for the first six months, your baby should always sleep in the same room as you (research shows it can reduce the incidence of crib death). However, a nursery is not based on purely practical considerations and inevitably you will want to set aside a room (if possible) to be considered your baby's own.

Ideally a nursery should be close to your own room. But there are also more esoteric considerations. So, before you choose the room, stop for a few moments (at least) and consider feng shui, the Chinese art of placement, which teaches that there are auspicious places for each room.

Feng shui evolved around five thousand years ago in China. The ancient Chinese believed that invisible life energy (called *qi*) flowed through everything in life. Centuries of observation showed that different areas of the house and different parts of each room attracted specific energies. Furthermore, they discovered that certain configurations (the layout of rooms or even the position of furniture or features) could either help or hinder the free, smooth flowing of energy. If the energy were blocked or allowed to flow too swiftly it would cause corresponding blockages and problems in life. Clutter can turn energy dull and stagnant. Sharp corners can send energy shooting out harshly. A series of open doors send energy racing through, too fast and frenzied. A blank wall will stop the energy dead. Fortunately, they also realized that very small but specific changes (known as "cures"), such as hanging wind chimes or crystals in certain places would correct such disharmony.

To find the best place for your nursery we need to look at the ba-gua. This is an octagonal template which divides any space (your entire home or simply a room within it) into eight areas. These eight areas (or corners) represent wealth, fame, marriage, children, helpful people, career, knowledge, and the family.

To work out the ba-gua, the position of the main door is important. If you live in an apartment or a single room you will need to take the door into your space as the main door, rather than the door that leads into the building as a whole. Now imagine yourself standing with your back to the door: depending on the position of the main door you will be standing in either the Knowledge, Career, or Helpful People corner of the ba-gua. Now envisage the ba-gua laid over your space. The Wealth corner will be off in the far left-hand corner, the Marriage corner in the far right-hand corner. The area we are most interested in, Children, will lie in the middle of the right-hand side, above Helpful People.

This position is where your nursery should ideally be situated. If this is impossible, don't worry but do ensure that the Children area of your house is kept clear, fresh, and uncluttered.

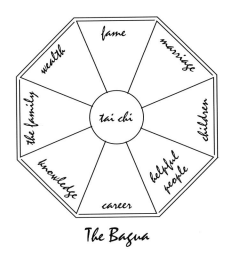

The Bagua

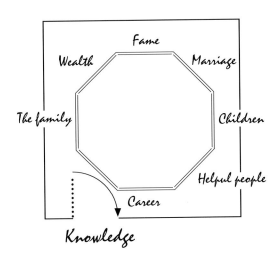

Knowledge

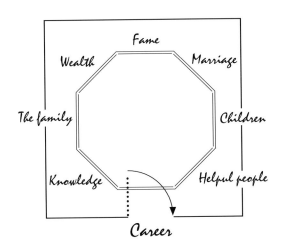

Career

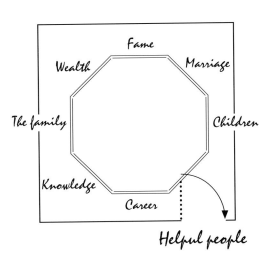

Helpful people

Positioning the crib

You can also apply the ba-gua to individual rooms. Lay it over your baby's nursery and see where each corner lies. If possible, you should place the cot or crib in the Children area of the room. If you cannot site the crib there, make sure this area is kept clean and place something white there (a pot of white flowers or a fluffy toy perhaps). Add a lamp to illuminate that area and energize it.

If you are sharing a room with your baby (or if your baby is sharing a room with an older sibling) you can use the ba-gua to discover the ideal spot for his or her crib.

Geopathic stress

Geopathic stress is believed to be caused by abnormal energy fields generated by deep underground streams, large mineral deposits, or faults in the substrata of the earth. It has been blamed as a major contributing factor in everything from migraines to cancer, from nightmares to divorce. Experiments have shown that bacteria grow abnormally when grown over underground currents of water; while mice inoculated with disease will fall ill far more rapidly when kept over a subterranean vein of water.

Obviously you want to be sure your nursery is free of geopathic stress—but don't panic. Geopathic stress moves in quite focused lines, so if the nursery were affected most likely you would just need to move the crib. To have your home tested you should find a dowser (one who has no interest in selling you anything). Professional dowsing societies may be able to put you in touch with someone local and reputable.

In the meantime, you can do some DIY detection.

- Dowsers say that typical signs of GS are feeling permanently tired and below par. Babies are fractious and difficult to settle. Children become disruptive and badly behaved (although there could be plenty of other reasons for that kind of behavior).

- Babies are very sensitive to GS. If your baby constantly rolls over to one corner of the crib he or she may be attempting to escape GS. Move the crib to another part of the room and see whether the baby stays put.
- You could also try putting cork tiles under the crib for a few weeks and see whether your baby starts to sleep better. The cork seems to neutralize the rays for a limited period. If they do start to feel better, try moving their bed.

Space cleansing

So you have picked your room. Before you jump in with a paintbrush; before you even start to dream up color schemes and wild murals for your nursery, you should spend some time cleansing the space on an energetic level.

It may sound silly, but every home and every room, however large or small, is far more than walls, roof, floor, and furniture. These factors generally stay put but there is another element to the home which is permanently shifting, moving, changing. This is the subtle energy of the home. Everything around us, whether it's a tree, a dog, or the kitchen table, is made up of vibrating energy fields. While the science remains mind-bogglingly baffling for most of us, we can all understand the theory in practice. If you've had a terrible argument, the room seems heavy and tense. We use the phrase "you could cut the air with a knife." The mood during a lively family meal is different again.

Imagine you hadn't physically cleaned a room for ten years. No dusting, no vacuuming, no window cleaning—nothing. Imagine what it would look and feel like. It's a pretty unpleasant thought, isn't it? Now think about one of the major rooms in your home. What has gone on in that room over the last ten years? You may have had good times there but equally you might have had rows, sat sobbing your heart out, felt depressed, or angry, or hopeless. Other people might have brought their negative feelings into that room. What about the people who lived there before you? How do you know what energy they left behind them? Now realize that you've only covered the last ten years. If you are living in an old building you could have decades, even centuries of hate, fear, loathing, malice, sadness, jealousy, resentment, and so forth built up like layers of grime. Of course you might be lucky and have happy, joyous feelings sticking to the walls. But, even so, you really don't want your baby living in someone else's atmosphere—far better to start afresh.

There is not space in this little book to go into space cleansing in great detail, but this basic space cleansing ceremony is perfectly adequate for the nursery. Just one note of caution—it is not advised to perform space cleansing while you are pregnant so if you are preparing your nursery before your baby is born you will need to enlist the help of a friend to do the cleansing.

1 Take a bath or shower. Add a couple of drops of rosemary oil (it helps to purify your aura.) Dress in clean, comfortable clothes but keep your feet bare and remove all jewelry and your watch.

2 Go to the center of the nursery and just stand there for a few moments with your eyes shut, quietly breathing and centering yourself. If you have any spiritual or religious beliefs you may like to say a prayer or ask your guardian angels or spirit animals for help.

3 Light a smudge stick or oil burner (add seven drops of lavender essential oil). Mentally or out loud, state your intention to purify and cleanse this space for your child. Use whatever words feel natural.

4 Now go around the whole space, sending smoke or the aromatherapy fumes into every room and corner of the home.

5 Next you will need to "clap out" the nursery. Move slowly and steadily around the room, clapping in every

7 Now you can go around the room balancing the energy by sounding a bell or a rattle. Imagine the sound clearing any last vestiges of old energy.

8 Return to the center of your space and once more close your eyes and breathe. How does the room feel now? Can you detect the difference?

9 Stamp your feet to ground yourself and have a good shake and stretch. It's a good idea to have something to eat and drink after this ritual.

corner. Clap your hands together, starting at the bottom of the wall and swiftly clapping on up towards the ceiling, as high as you can. You may need to repeat several times in each spot—until the sound of your clapping becomes clear. As you clap, visualize your clapping dispersing all the stagnant old energy.

6 When you have finished wash your hands.

You can repeat this ceremony whenever you feel the need. It's particularly useful after illness or any form of upset or argument. Babies are incredibly sensitive to atmospheres and so a quick space cleanse can make a huge difference. However, when using smudge sticks, incense, or oils make sure your baby is not in the room and stays out of it for several hours afterwards.

Spirit of Safety

Is your nursery a safe space for your delicate child? It's ironic that many parents, acting out of purely the best intentions, may unwittingly be preparing a toxic nightmare for their baby. Recent reports indicate that we are exposed to up to 300 volatile organic (carbon-based) compounds within the home. It is thought that tens of thousands of cancer deaths annually are brought about by indoor air pollutants—the hoard of chemicals which may be quietly seeping into our homes. Sadly the greatest threat is from new materials—paint, soft furnishings, carpets, furniture, wallpaper (exactly what you may well be planning for that gorgeous new nursery).

It's a very real concern as babies are far more vulnerable than adults to toxins. They are smaller and have faster respiratory and metabolic rates, so they can ingest pollutants far more easily and swiftly, and the build-up in the body is more concentrated.

Don't panic though—you can make the nursery both look good and be safe. Here's how...

Best basics

Floor coverings

Avoid synthetic foam-backed carpets. Instead choose washable floors of recycled wood or untreated lino or cork— these are ideal as they are non-toxic and hygienic. They also look great and are easily cleaned (and trust me, that is important). Pure white carpet may look gorgeous but think ahead and imagine its pure gorgeousness with a liberal splattering of baby goo and slime! Linoleum is now very fashionable and incredibly hygienic—and it comes in a host of colors and patterns. If you feel it may be a bit cold and hard, you could add a cheerful rug (see left) for color and warmth.

Natural floor coverings such as sisal, coir, seagrass, and jute look good and are non-toxic but can be harsh on tender knees and are horrors to clean (you try

picking out play-dough from seagrass—
I have and I don't recommend it. If you
want to go for carpet, 100 percent wool
or cotton/wool mix carpets and rugs are
an option, but don't expect to keep them
looking pristine. Many companies now
produce stunning natural fabric rugs for
children (some come looking like
squashed but friendly dogs, cats, and
cows) or you could choose a zebra print
for early visual stimulation, or fake
cowhide for a western look. Note:
patterns are a *very* good idea as spills
and stains are less noticeable.

Paints

Look out for paints which are water-,
milk-, plant-, and mineral-based. The
days when you could only find variations
on magnolia or sludge-green are long
gone and many of them have a lovely
powdery matt finish as a bonus. The
downside is that they aren't as mark-
resistant as your average vinyl matt (but
you can usually mix in a water-based
varnish for a tougher finish). If you want
vibrant colors use powdered pigments
which you simply mix yourself. Old-
fashioned milk paints are long-lasting,
safe, and come in a huge range of
fashionable and traditional colors.
Pick natural thinners, such as linseed oil
and pine resin turpentine, and choose
natural varnishes which allow the wood
to breathe (they combine resins with
scented turpentine and pigments).
The added benefit is that, unlike ordinary
varnishes, they smell lovely.

Furniture

When buying new furniture you really do need to be careful. Check which materials are used in the stuffing, base, and fabric of chairs. Be very wary of treated materials—they may prevent stains but could be nasty to your health (think instead about loose covers which can easily be washed). Recycled wood is a great option for nursery furniture—if you can track down someone who works with it. Or try to find craftspeople who use untreated wood from sustainable sources. Check out local carpenters and crafts guilds—it probably won't work out more expensive and you will have totally unique furniture. Second-hand cribs are a great idea. If you have a family heirloom so much the better (but do check it for safety as older models may not meet current standards). It needs to be sturdy enough that it won't fall over when your baby is old enough to stand up. Also check that the bars aren't so far apart that your baby could get stuck between them. If the sides come down they need to be able to be locked so the baby can't undo them.

Don't be sniffy about buying your crib second-hand. We naturally want the best for our babies and in most people's mind that means new—and not somebody's cast-off. But in the case of nursery furniture leave aside your prejudices and scour the small ads. Of course it goes without saying that you should clean any second-hand crib very thoroughly (with non-toxic cleaners). I would also give it a lovely fresh new coat of paint (using natural healthy paints of course—see above) so it looks fresh and inviting.

If you really can't bear not to have a new crib try to buy one which hasn't been varnished or treated (a tall order). If this isn't possible, buy it way in advance and, if possible, leave outdoors or in a garage until you need it.

Fabrics

Pick 100 percent natural fibers for curtains, covers, and particularly bedlinen. This can be a tough one as every baby store and catalog is packed to the gills with vibrant tempting fabrics, curtains, and linen. But what's most important—design or safety? Okay, trendy designer mothers out there—don't answer that one.

Some people feel that curtains can attract dust and so aren't great news for babies. Certainly it's a good idea to keep your window treatments on the unfussy side, rather than choosing yards upon yards of flounces and frills. An alternative is to eschew curtains altogether and opt for blinds. I chose simple wooden slatted louvre blinds for my son's bedroom— they look fabulous, can easily be wiped clean, and also have various options: full black-out, lifted up for total daylight, or with the slats open for a soft twilight effect (ideal for daytime naps). One word of warning—ensure that you hook any strings out of reach of small hands.

Organic unbleached cotton makes the most wonderful sheets and duvet covers (for older children) as it gets softer and softer the more you wash it. In hot weather, cool linen sheets are about the most inviting fabric you could put on your baby's bed. Cotton cellular blankets (buy a few so you can layer them if it's cold) are fine but wash them before use. However tempting it may be, do avoid using fabric conditioners—they aren't necessary and may cause allergies.

General hints for a safe nursery

- Keep the nursery as well aired and ventilated as possible. Open the windows and let the air in—for at least fifteen minutes twice a day. This also helps to prevent excess humidity and stops the air from becoming stale.
- Avoid air conditioning if you can: install window and ceiling fans to keep the air cool.
- Always use natural cleaning products.
- Get rid of any fluorescent lights and replace lightbulbs where possible with full spectrum light.
- If you live in an area with radon, do have your home checked and take advice if radon is found—it can be a killer.
- Fit safety covers over all electrical sockets or have them repositioned high on the walls.
- If your nursery does have some toxic threats, fill it with healing plants before your baby takes up residence. Choose from peace lilies, dwarf banana plants, golden pothos, peperomias, spider plants, mother-in-law's tongue (sanseviera), Chinese evergreens (agloanema), and goosefoot plants (syngonium podophyllum).

Spirit of Color

Blue for a boy, pink for a girl. Color assumptions are there from the word go. But which colors *should* you choose for your baby's nursery? We tend to follow tradition—soft, pastel colors are almost *de rigueur*.

Rita Alexander, of the International Association for Color explains that the choice of blue and pink is actually (and mostly unintentionally, at least nowadays) a way of balancing the male and female aspects of our being. "We dress little girls in pink which is in effect red (Mars, the male energy)," she says, "and little boys in blue (the female moon energy). Unconsciously we are effecting a balance through color."

Color therapists often disagree on precisely which colors are suitable for young babies. But generally the consensus is that pale soft colors are ideal. This is based more on spiritual principles than anything rigorously scientific. In point of fact, the cones (the light receptors in the eye that give color vision) are not well enough developed in the newborn to see color. This is why many "educational toys" for newborns and young babies use starkly contrasting colors or tones (such as the black and white Lamaze designs). Personally I'm not a huge fan of trying to educate your child while he or she is still in nappies (or in the womb) but if you're keen to bring up the next Einstein then you'll find lots of vivid mobiles and flash cards in black and white.

I have to say I think color should be used more gently. Rudolf Steiner, the great spiritual thinker, believed that young babies should be surrounded by rosy pinks, mauve, soft blue, sunny yellow, or creamy white tones. His suggestion was that you should buy two silk veils, one blue and the other pink

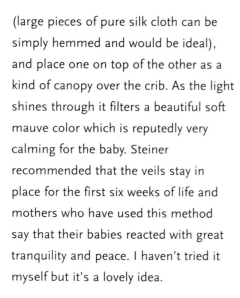

Pink for a boy, blue for a girl?

(large pieces of pure silk cloth can be simply hemmed and would be ideal), and place one on top of the other as a kind of canopy over the crib. As the light shines through it filters a beautiful soft mauve color which is reputedly very calming for the baby. Steiner recommended that the veils stay in place for the first six weeks of life and mothers who have used this method say that their babies reacted with great tranquility and peace. I haven't tried it myself but it's a lovely idea.

Many parents have the dilemma that they simply don't know what sex child they are having and don't want to saddle little Alice with a blue bedroom or little Thomas with Barbie pink. Frankly I think it doesn't matter one iota but I can see traditionalists shaking their heads in horror at the idea.

Fortunately there are plenty of other options. My personal choice fell on a buttery soft but sure yellow for my son's nursery. It is sunny and cheery—also very useful as it brightens up a room which doesn't get the sun all day long. Yellow works well for boys and girls and is cheery for parents too. Don't forget that you are going to be the main one observing your color choices so do pick something *you* like.

If you're a bit of a minimalist, maybe look at lovely soft creams and vanilla shades. You can then introduce color and warmth with your accessories. Soft lilac is also another good option and lovely for either sex as it sits mid-way between pink and blue.

Remember it isn't written in stone that you have to paint every wall the same color. It can be very effective to have just one wall in a scrumptious shade, and the others in toning shades of something neutral like ivory. Or what's to stop you painting one wall pink, one blue, one yellow, one white? Or mark off stripes of varying widths with tape and go stripy. Or paint a gingham effect.

Wallpapers

There are plenty of choices for nurseries in the wallpaper books of various designers. Most are quite traditional but some are a bit more adventurous. Simple graphic patterns such as spots, flowers, and stripes can be effective. Some companies also have quirky designs such as topiary and desert scenes. Toile de Jouy can look very effective in a traditional house's nursery—but don't overdo it. Again, you don't have to smother your room in a riot of pattern. You could paper just one wall and paint the others. This can work well if you have a large pattern.

One important point. Your baby really won't mind if you paper the walls with scenes from Bosch or Bruegel but as babies turn into toddlers they become hyper-aware of what's around them. What looks innocuous in the broad light of day can turn into terrifying monsters come nightfall and darkness. I remember being terrified of the shapes that emerged from my wallpaper in twilight. Evil faces seemed to peer out where sweet flowers had bloomed during the day. So be careful if you intend your choices to last your child into toddlerdom and beyond.

Colored Accessories

Accessories are a wonderful way to introduce bright oases of color into a nursery. Let's brainstorm a few ideas:

- Think about vibrant cushions in fabulous clashing colors (fabrics like wool, felt, and cotton work well). Babies love texture so how about incorporating some velvet, silk, fake fur, or hessian?
- Pictures and posters are an inexpensive way of introducing color, but you don't have to limit yourself to these— how about mounting a beautiful rug or blanket on the wall.

- Hang crystals in the window and let rainbows dance all around your nursery. Babies are totally mesmerized by them.
- Colored glass filters light in an entrancing way. Put colored glasses on a glass shelf—but keep it high and remove as soon as your baby starts to explore and reach high.
- How about painting a design on the upper panes of a nursery window (you can buy glass paints from art shops), or commission a stained glass mosaic (but don't forget to consider how it will look in the dark).

Aura Soma

Aura Soma is a form of color therapy—
you may have seen the beautiful dual-
colored bottles in intoxicating color
combinations. They are made up of pure
base oils and spring water with herbs
and flower essences added. Once again,
these look lovely against the light if
placed in a window. Choose the one or
ones to which you are intuitively drawn. If
you're pregnant, try placing them against
your tummy to see if your baby moves to
any of them. There is one specific bottle
designed for babies and children: Star
Child (or Child Rescue), which is royal
blue above pale pink. The color
combination is said to balance the male
and female aspects of our being. It's a
gentle, soothing remedy which might
even be helpful for teething and is great
for calming nightmares in older babies
and toddlers.

Spirit of Scent

The sense of smell is incredibly powerful. A newborn baby will know its mother by her smell alone and can even detect if a woman is lactating. Equally, a mother can sniff out her baby blindfold among a gaggle of infants. No surprise then that you should treat your baby's nose with great respect.

Virtually every baby product you come across is "scented" or "fragranced." Maybe lightly scented but still scented— and usually with horrible synthetic perfumes. I just don't get it. Why do we try to disguise the smell of our babies?

Yes, a full nappy isn't the most beguiling scent on the planet and I won't be racing to market "baby posset" as a fragrance but those are about the only unpleasant pongs and very transient ones at that. Also, and trust me on this one, however sensitive your nose (and stomach) you will always be able to deal with your own baby's poo (I think it's one of those examples of Nature being incredibly smart). But most of these products aren't even aimed at combating nappy-pong. They are all designed to make your baby's skin and hair (if he or she possesses any) smell "nice." Personally I don't think there are many smells to beat that of pure fresh unadorned baby skin. It's divine—right up there with freshly mown lawns and dew on flowers. Why cover it up?

Equally, why put fragrance on fragile skin and assault your baby's sensitive nose? Even the most carefully produced "pediatrician-approved" baby products have a long list of quite unpleasant chemicals in them. Frankly, what is wrong with pure fresh water? My son had very sensitive, eczema-prone skin and I found that one of the prerequisites for keeping his skin clear was to avoid absolutely anything with synthetic scents (and other chemical additives). If your baby has very dry skin you can use a tiny amount of pure virgin organic olive oil for lubrication—baby creams and lotions are usually packed full of nasties. So too are baby wipes—use a muslin and water

instead at home (I confess I resort to wipes for ease while out).

Equally, do try to avoid synthetic softeners and conditioners when washing baby clothes and bed linen. They really aren't necessary at all and can cause allergic skin reactions. Use the very gentlest washing powder you can find—simple soap suds are best. If your baby has very sensitive skin it is well worth putting everything twice through a rinse cycle so that all traces of washing powder are removed.

Remember that the most comforting smell of all for a baby is that of its mother. Leaving you is the biggest step a baby can take so prepare for this before your baby is born. Almost all children have a comfort object of some description which they will take from babyhood through the toddler years (and sometimes way beyond). You can't ever dictate what this object might be but you

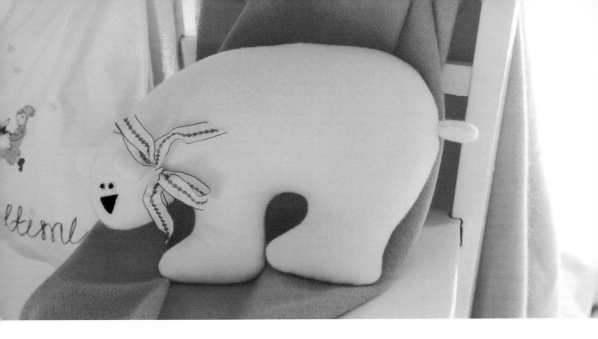

can have a decent stab at getting your baby fixated on an item of your choice, rather than a ragged piece of old muslin.

Take your chosen snugly, blanket, or comfort toy to bed with you for a few nights, cuddle it close to your heart and allow your scent to infuse it. You may also like to visualize that you are putting all your love and protection and feelings of safety and warmth into it for your baby. Then, when you have turned it into almost an amulet of love and peace, give it to your baby who will most probably find it incredibly comforting. Of course there will always be one who will toss it aside without a moment's thought—so don't be offended if your love offering is spurned (it's all in the nature of babies and small children).

Aromatherapy

Safe scents for the nursery

Aromatherapy can be used with wonderful effect on children. However, if you have a very young baby you must be very careful— aromatherapists tend to stick to just lavender or Roman camomile oils as they are very gentle. Even so, use them very sparingly and never undiluted on bare skin. You can put one drop of each in a cup of milk and add to a bath to aid relaxation.

Researchers have found that if you let someone smell lavender and then take an EEG (electroencephalogram), it will show increased alpha brain wave activity. Alpha brain waves are those which promote a relaxed, calm state of mind. So, if your baby is restless or seems distressed, you can try placing a bowl of steaming water with just one drop of lavender essential oil or Roman camomile under the foot of the crib. This will also help if your baby is congested or has difficulty breathing.

Baby massage

One of the loveliest things you can do with your baby is to massage him or her. Research clearly shows that touch, and massage in particular, can help babies grow—both physically and emotionally. It's also a superb way of learning how to bond with your baby. Not everyone feels that instant attachment to their baby and, particularly if you have suffered or are suffering from one of the various forms of post-natal depression, it can be quite difficult to feel close and natural with your baby. This is not your fault so please don't get yourself into a state of guilt and self-recrimination. You are not a bad mother. There isn't room in a book this size to go into this issue but do seek help if you feel anxious, depressed, or just "not right"—your physician can help. Research has also found that baby massage can be incredibly useful for both mother and baby in this instance.

Many hospitals, medical centers, and natural health clinics now run courses in

infant massage. But you and your baby can really learn your own way.

1 Make up your massage oil. Add 1–2 drops of lavender and/or Roman camomile oil to 2 tbsp/30ml of sweet almond oil and gently shake to disperse. Use organic oils if possible. Decant the oil into a clean bottle (you won't need all this oil for one massage so keep it in a cool place for future massages).

2 Make sure your baby is warm and in a good mood—introduce massage for the first few times only when your baby is relaxed and happy (later on when it is common practice you will find it might help when he or she is fractious or upset).

3 Put a tiny bit of oil on your hands and rub together so they are warm.

4 Gently stroke your baby's body—working from the extremities (toes and fingers) towards the heart (this is the direction the blood flows). Pay attention to your baby's back, legs and toes, arms and hands. Make gentle clockwise circling movements on the baby's abdomen.

5 Don't be tempted to try "classic" massage techniques or anything deep or strong—be very very gentle.

6 Keep your early massage sessions short and sweet. In other words, quit while you're ahead. Five minutes will be plenty.

Your baby will swiftly become accustomed to the soothing scent of your chosen aromatherapy oils. You can use this to your advantage if you have to leave your baby with a relative or carer. Leave a tissue with a little bit of your massage oil on it with the person looking after your baby. If the baby becomes distressed at all, a swift sniff may prove to be comforting enough to calm him or her down.

Space essences

I have recently been delighted to find that many of the major flower essence companies have introduced special room sprays that combine the gentle power of flower essences with that of aromatherapy. Use these sprays to cleanse and spiritually clear your nursery—you can use them in space cleansing ceremonies (see page 12) and blessings (page 81) or simply as a swift, effective way of bringing a gentle, loving atmosphere to your nursery.

Some of my favorites include:
- Space Clearing by Australian Bush Flower Essences
- Sanctuary by Findhorn Flower Essences
- Purification by Alaskan Essences
- Heart Spirit Spray by Pacific Essences
- Angel Rejuvenation by Star Flower Essences
- White Beauty Aura Spray by Living Tree Essences

There is also a lovely spray called Calling All Angels by Alaskan Essences which was specifically designed with children in mind—to combat nightmares. Newborn babies don't have nightmares as far as we know but I love the idea of calling down guardian angels to guard a baby's crib.

Use these essences when your baby isn't in the room and leave the room for a few hours before bringing your baby in. Spray into the corners of the room and give a very light spritz (and no more) over the crib.

Spirit of Sound

Babies hear everything. Okay, they might not understand every word (although sometimes I'm not even so sure about that) but they will most certainly pick up on the meaning from your tone and your mood. So do try your hardest not to have arguments in front of your baby, or shout or swear, or say anything negative. Although older children can benefit from seeing how adults cope with disagreements, a baby simply doesn't have the necessary comprehension—they just absorb the psychic stress and hate it.

Once again the experts are divided on what sounds a young baby should hear. The Steiner approach is that mechanical sounds such as vacuum cleaners, washing machines, and (sin of sins) the television are absolutely horrendous. Instead, mothers should sing lullabies or softly play the lyre or flute. Now, that's just fine if you happen to have a spare flute handy but I have to say my flute or lyre-playing would be guaranteed to send any baby into a tantrum of tiny-fisted fury. Having said that, if you do play a musical instrument then how lovely to be able to soothe your baby to sleep with the sound of violin or piano, cello or oboe. My husband used to sit and quietly play his guitar to James, who adored the sound. I wasn't so keen but always gave a quiet prayer of thanks that I hadn't married a drummer.

Of course, if you go into any baby shop you'll be inundated with machines and gizmos which will sing to your baby, play sounds to your baby, coo nursery rhymes at your baby. For the most part, they are pretty ghastly—cloying and synthetic. I hate to say it but I think it's another way we are opting out of childcare. I've even heard of people who tuck their children up and then turn on a tape for their bedtime story. No, no, no—sorry but I do think we have a duty to sit and sing to our children and later on to read to them. Duty is maybe the wrong word as it implies it's a chore—in point of fact, sharing a bedtime song or book is just the loveliest way of getting close to a child. Please don't use the excuse that you can't sing or are a lousy narrator of tales—a baby can hardly be classed as an exacting audience.

I have to say that I'm with Steiner on lullabies. They really *are* lovely. Lullabies are the archetypal songs of babyhood, an unbroken link with our mothers and grandmothers, and reach way back into the mists of time. They not only soothe the baby but, often more importantly, soothe the parent or babysitter too (and heaven knows, we need soothing). Lullabies are curious entitie.

Some are supremely protective and act almost as a magic charm to ward off evil:

Sleep my little one, sleep;
fond vigil I keep.

Others are quite the opposite:

Rock-a-bye baby on the tree top,
When the wind blows the cradle will rock;
When the bough breaks, the cradle will fall,
Down will come baby, cradle and all.

Maybe the idea is that, by voicing the worst, we can prevent it from happening, which makes sense when you think how anxious new parents are about their children. Throughout myth and folklore there is an obsessive need and urge to protect babies and children. The Greek Achilles was placed in the river of

immortality—but held by his heel (which became the only vulnerable part of his body). The Norse God Baldur was given blessings over his cradle which recited all the metals and woods from which he would be protected—yet they failed to include mistletoe (which of course proved his undoing).

If you don't remember the lullabies your own mother sang to you, sing the songs you love yourself (James used to get my old Girl Guide songs when I ran out of lullabies). Anything soft and repetitious has the desired effect. Don't worry if your singing voice leaves a lot to be desired—your baby won't mind. If you really can't sing, then hum. Soft gentle humming is supremely soothing —for both hummer and baby. It's particularly useful if you're feeling anxious and stressed.

However, many modern researchers say that Steiner and the lullaby merchants have got it all wrong. Although lullabies are fine and dandy, so too are everyday noises. A baby is used to mechanical sounds, they insist, and in actual fact they will be soothed by vacuum cleaners and washing machines, televisions and lawnmowers. The theory runs that monotonous sounds are the best at soothing babies—and what is more monotonous than the drone of a vacuum cleaner? Also, babies pick up sounds in the womb (albeit muffled) and so are used to a wide range of domestic noises. This does seem to be true. There are the classic tales of women who watched TV soaps during their pregnancies only to find that their babies, once born, cooed contentedly and relaxed as soon as the theme tunes began to

play. Certainly my own son dances around to the theme tune of my husband's favorite radio show.

Babies do seem to like to hear sounds around them. Everyday noise and hubbub seem to be relaxing to a baby—perhaps because it reassures them that there are people around. I would suggest you try out a variety of sounds and see which appeal to your baby. Some people have found that recording the spin cycle of the washing machine over and over has given hours of peaceful slumber. Others swear by Mozart, Gregorian Chant, or Madonna. Who cares? If it works, go for it.

Just one caveat to that. If you want to retain your sanity, don't get into the habit of playing nursery rhymes in the car. Babies frankly don't give a damn what's on the radio so you can play your favorite music (rock, classical, folk, hardcore) with complete impunity—though try not to deafen your baby.

Sounds of nature

I think it's a nice idea to introduce your baby to as many natural sounds as possible. Once they get to a few months old, they will start to notice sounds and may even coo delightedly at the sound of birdsong or the wind in the trees. Let's think of a few ways of doing this:

- Very gentle wind chimes are lovely in a baby's room but choose with care. You're after the gentlest tinkle, not a crashing cacophony.
- Ocean sounds or whale song can be incredibly soothing and relaxing.
- Soft drum beats and chanting are almost hypnotic—most New Age shops can provide a selection.
- Intrauterine sounds have been researched in many nurseries and have been found to create soothing, comforting effects in newborns.

- Leave a window open so your baby can hear the birds, the soft rain, the wind (and yes, even the traffic).
- Install a waterfall feature in the nursery, not only is the sound of water soothing but it's great feng shui too. Obviously you will have to move it when your baby starts to explore (or put it on a high shelf, making sure there aren't hanging leads).

By the way, the one exception to the "banish electronic gizmos" rule of mine is a baby monitor. If your baby is even remotely out of earshot a baby monitor is an absolute necessity. Just remember that it's not just baby you can hear but anyone in the close vicinity so don't get caught out with indiscrete conversation—many a gossiper has been red-faced on realizing their comments were broadcast to all and sundry.

Furniture and Furnishings

What do you need for a baby's nursery? If you believe the baby stores and catalogs, a baby needs more furniture than the rest of the family put together. But actually your child's needs are few.

Cribs and cradles

A baby needs somewhere to sleep. But that somewhere could be almost anywhere snug and safe. Full-size cribs threaten to engulf a small baby and most people feel uneasy about placing a tiny bundle in a sea of bedclothes. So for the first few months most people tend to plump for either a Moses basket or a small (often rocking) crib. These are lovely choices and offer the perfect chance to indulge any fairy-tale urges you have for swathes of billowing muslin or folkloric rocking cradles.

Symbolically, the cradle is the cosmic barque, the ship of life rocking on the primordial ocean. It is a potent symbol of new life and fresh beginnings. Those with a macabre turn of mind may reflect that the wooden cradle ushers us into the

world while the wooden coffin takes us out—two boat-like structures in which to float our souls.

Nowadays you can buy lovely cribs in unusual materials, such as metal or even Perspex. But to my mind a crib is always fashioned of wood. Even the Moses basket should, I think, be kept in traditional basketwork, twined with living withies. Wood lives. It is also regarded as having special healing and protective properties and, traditionally, only certain woods were used to fashion the baby's crib. Beverly Pagram, author of *Hearth and Home* (Gaia Books), says it should be oak, a "pagan protective tree." The rocking cradle was once hung with amulets fashioned from rowan and hawthorn which are considered emblems of fertility, birth, and protection (all tied with some anti-witchcraft red thread). Hawthorn is also thought to be a healing tree for children and it used to be common to tie hawthorn blossoms to the baby's cradle for protection and healing.

Cedar is another highly protective wood for children and babies. It is closely associated with the Babylonian mother goddess Ishtar and is generally considered to be protective, and to confer abundance. In the Native American tradition, cedarwood is also considered protective and is burned at blessing ceremonies for babies and children. The other tree intimately connected with cradles is birch. In the Celtic tradition, birch is the tree of birth, of springtime, and new beginnings so no wonder birch wood was sought for cribs.

Most rocking cribs sit on the floor but you might also think about suspending your crib from the ceiling (from a very firm hook embedded in a rafter). This can look absolutely enchanting and certainly makes the crib into a design statement all of its own.

Of course, many people dispense with crib or basket altogether and have their baby in the bed with them. Childcare experts advise against it on the whole stating that it slightly increases the risk of SIDS, or crib death. However, traditional peoples (and those who couldn't afford cribs) have always done it and other experts furiously assert that it's the most natural and best place for baby to be. Personally I think the new breed of cribs which have a collapsible side (so you can push it right up against your bed) are a great compromise. You get your own space (and trust me a baby can push you out of bed just as easily as a large person) and if you need to comfort your baby or feed him or her you're just an arm-length away.

As your baby grows, a full-size crib becomes necessary and you will need to take care about stringent safety instructions (see Chapter Two). A baby doesn't need and shouldn't have a pillow (for fear of suffocation), and keep bedding simple. Bumpers are just another potential source of suffocation as far as I can see (as well as being perennially ugly). One of the best-ever items I invested in was a sleeping bag with arms in it (you pop your baby in and he or she can't possibly wriggle out of the covers). It's ideal if you live in a cold climate.

Beyond that lies the siren-lure of the proper bed. Resist it as long as you possibly can. Once your child is in a bed you no longer have them caged and safe. I would honestly say your best bet is to keep your child in a crib until he or she either regularly climbs (and falls) out of it or their feet start to stick through the

bars at the end. Then and only then think bed. Shortly after that think safety. A small futon makes a safe place if your child makes an early transition—or take the mattress off the bed and put it on the floor (airing it frequently). Sleigh beds make great first beds as they have high sides. Equally practical but not as stylish is a portable barrier which holds small people in bed.

Whether crib or bed, let your imagination run wild with colors and decoration. I once saw the most magical bed, made up to look like something from a fairy tale (perhaps the Princess and the Pea). It was painted red and gold with the little girl's name on it, along with a very regal crown. My son James insisted on having a blue bed, so we bought a plain untreated pine bed and duly "colored it in" (as James put it). How about a star-spangled bed or a stripy crib? A zebra bed or a spotty crib?

Changing tables

If I've gone on and on about cribs and beds it's purely because you really don't need much else in the way of furniture for your nursery. Somewhere to change your baby is great but it's not strictly necessary. A mat on the floor will do just dandy. However, if you suffer from backache, having everything at a comfortable height will be a boon. But it need not be a shop-bought changing table—most are hideous and cost a fortune. Instead haul an old chest of drawers into service.

We used a big old chest and simply tapped in a guard rail all around then plonked a changing mat on top with some adhesive pads to keep it from sliding around. Screw in a hook on one side and hang from it one of those organizers with lots of pockets for nappies, wipes, bags etc. Suspend a fascinating mobile above it—or stick a bright picture or pattern on the ceiling to keep your baby intrigued while you attend to the business end. Put a nappy bin on the other side and you're sorted.

Storage

You'll be amazed how baby stuff proliferates. It just grows and grows and before long you're tripping over teddies, bricks, and general baby detritus. While your baby is small, a toy box will do the trick. You can paint it, painstakingly letter or stencil it, and generally make it beautiful. It could be a Pirate's treasure chest, a mossy stump of a tree, a fairy's hoard... (make sure the lid won't slam shut on tender fingers though—stick-on cushioning will do). Most of your baby's things, however, will be so gorgeous you will have them out on display on shelves or sitting lined up on chairs or mantelpieces. It's only as your baby transmutes into a toddler and develops fixations on horrible cartoon characters and space rockets that good storage becomes not only necessary but imperative. Some of the best systems offer a low-level line of pull-out compartments (either in wood, plastic, or fabric). Low-level offers good access for your child and lots of compartments means you can separate out the rails from the rockets, Barbie from the bricks.

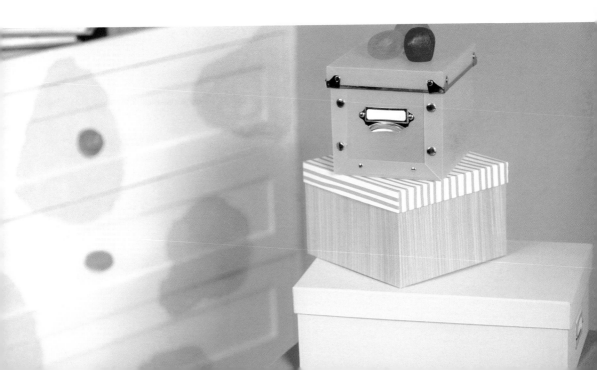

A rocking chair

So much for baby gently rocking; how about you? For the first few years one of the absolute essentials for a nursery is a really comfortable chair for the parent or carer. A rocking chair is ideal for nursing, cuddling, and story-reading but, if you plump for a lovely old wooden one, make sure you pad it well with a plump cushion and a rug for your back—they can be quite uncomfortable in the long term. This really is a case where you should go for function rather than looks. A big comfy armchair is bliss—and you can cover it with loose coverings (useful as it's bound to get sticky finger stains over it).

My only other absolute "must-have" is a sheepskin rug. You can buy ones which have been scrupulously sterilized and even ones with carefully positioned openings so you can use it in your buggy. A sheepskin is warm and cosy and comforting for babies. We used ours as a portable comforter—to give continuity when we were away from home. Some people advocate them in cribs but I kept it for out-of-crib snoozes and to keep away drafts. They machine wash too.

Spirit of Fun

This is the fun chapter. Well, most of them are fun but above all I really think that it's the details that make a great nursery—and it's the details that are the most fun.

Babies have a great sense of humor. They laugh at anything remotely incongruous and often at anything else as well. Frankly there is no better sound than that of a baby or small child chuckling or giggling, so take every opportunity you can to induce a smile. I'm not suggesting you turn your nursery into a cartoon gallery—but this is one occasion when you can use whimsy, imagination, and fun in bucketloads. So why not indulge?

Wall decorations

It used to be *de rigueur* to have fancy borders around the nursery. It's a swift way to introduce playful elements but the choice is usually limited and can look a little old-fashioned now. If you are wedded to nursery rhyme characters or cartoon characters then maybe investigate some of the new stick-on and peel-off figures which are available.

The brilliant thing about these is that you can easily shift them around as your baby grows (my son's Maisie figures started off marching around above the skirting board but are now hovering out of reach near the ceiling. Equally, you can take them off without pulling away half your wallpaper

when allegiances change—and change they do. I fear poor Maisie is soon to be usurped by Thunderbirds.

If you're wildly talented yourself or are willing to pay someone to do it for you, then think about a mural. There are some absolutely incredible professional

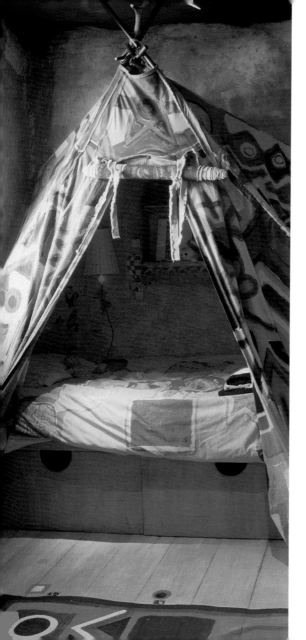

muralists around who will indulge your wildest fantasies. They could transform the whole room into a fairy castle or Pooh Bear's house; they might wave their magic paintbrushes and leave you with a jungle of a nursery or an enchanted forest. Before you take the plunge do remember a few things: firstly, it will be very expensive; secondly, it may well be a bit overwhelming; thirdly, you will be heartbroken when your child gets older and turns round and says they hate it. If you can cope with the idea that it won't be forever and that there will come the day when you'll be wallpapering over it, then fine, go ahead.

Alternatively, you could opt for something less obtrusive. I've seen incredible trompe l'oeil effects that are just stunning—an imaginary window with a garden or cityscape behind, a fireplace with a friendly cat sitting in front of it, a shelf filled with toys and books etc.

Of course, you can always have a go yourself. It need not be too complicated. An azure blue ceiling studded with moon and stars is within the reach of even the least artistic. Simple graphic shapes which can be drawn with a ruler can be gently shunted into exciting shapes such as trains, cars, playhouses. Remind yourself of your old childhood skills such as tracing and copying. Trace around a favorite image in a book, enlarge it, and transfer to your wall. Simple is good as far as babies are concerned. They will love a simple line of brightly colored balls bouncing along a wall, and adore dogs and cats with wobbly legs and big ears.

As I've already mentioned, whatever your wall coverings give them the "in the dark" test. This goes for mobiles and pictures too. I bought James a gorgeous flying dragon that hung over his babyhood crib. As he grew older he started getting distressed when he went to bed. I couldn't figure it out until one night I lay down on the floor (in exhausted parent pose) and looked up. In the dark, the dragon hung ominously like a predatory bat. I took it down and James slept just fine. Multiply that effect by ten for a jungle scene—unless it's done very carefully.

Mobiles

Let's take a look at mobiles. Rare is the nursery without at least one—for two very good reasons:

1 Movement fascinates babies.
2 Babies are stuck on their backs most of the time.

Ergo, it makes perfect sense to give them something fun to look at, positioned just where they can see it. Whenever you get the chance, let your baby look at some real-life natural mobiles—trees. There is nothing more fascinating for a baby than to watch the shifting light, the gently moving leaves. Ferret around for really lovely and unusual mobiles. Craft shops and traditional toy shops are often good sources.

One lovely thing to do is to make what I call a "medicine" mobile. In Native American tradition, a medicine bag or bundle is a way of carrying the sacred with you at all times; it is filled with powerful meaningful objects and is a symbol of the deep inner self. A medicine mobile can give protection and peace to your baby. Make it mindfully and choose your objects with care. You might like to use some of the following:

- Bright, beautiful beads threaded onto embroidery thread or very fine strips of hide.
- Small crystals (wind a little jewelry wire around them in a spiral to keep them encased and then suspend from ribbon or hide.)
- Special stones, shells, and pieces of driftwood (attach as for crystals.)
- A small dream catcher.
- Feathers.
- Strips of bright cloth.

Make your initial structure out of rowan if you can (for its protective qualities).

There are plenty of other things that can hang over a crib and provide both amusement and spiritual protection for your baby. A Brigid cross is made of two pieces of rowan wood lashed together and then woven with rainbow pieces of thread or wool. Some people add beads or feathers according to how the spirit moves them. The Brigid, or Bride, cross is a symbol of St Brigid, who is patroness of childbirth and protectress of small children (as well as love and warmth for the home) so it's a lovely symbol. You might also think about painting a series of mandalas and suspending them about the crib. Or how about blowing and then painting eggs for an Easter mobile.

Lights and lanterns

A light fitting is another excuse for something interesting on the ceiling. Who says a lampshade needs to be the classic "hat" shape? Why not have a sheep-shaped lampshade, or a dragon, or a rabbit or, well, anything really (you can buy these ready-made or if you're clever—though do watch out for safety—make one yourself). Simple yet still effective is to take a large spherical paper lantern and decorate it to resemble a globe, or a beach ball, or Humpty Dumpty. Or stick pieces of colored tissue paper around it in jewel-colors so you get a stained glass effect. Moroccan or Indian jeweled and stained-glass lanterns would throw gorgeous colors around the room too.

Table-top lanterns come in all shapes and designs now—most lovely of all are the ones which project colored shapes onto the walls. Babies adore the movement and find them incredibly soothing. I'd be wary of intricate tableau lanterns of fairy glens and so on—babies won't appreciate them and as they get older they will simply want to maul them. Simple graphic shapes are better. Again there are stand-alone animals which are good fun. You can also buy a simple paper lantern (some are huge—hurrah!—who says nursery lighting has to be teensy?) that you can decorate with your own designs. Try something bold: zebra stripes maybe, or leopard spots—or stick on large colored splodges or circles.

Night lights are synonymous with childhood but some experts now warn that babies and children should sleep in the dark as it is better for their eyes. If your baby is unperturbed by the dark

(and be careful you don't project your own fears onto him or her) then I would certainly let him or her sleep in the velvety darkness. However, I really don't believe it's right to force darkness on a terrified child and in such cases a small night light can be very comforting (and my honest belief is that it won't do much harm). Use a natural flame rather than a low-level electric light and make sure it is totally safe (i.e. in a solid container and somewhere it can't be knocked over). If you're as neurotic as I am, place it in a shallow bowl of sand or water for complete safety. Make sure no pets can get in to knock it over.

A jelly-jar painted with glass paint can make a great holder—and the colors will glow pleasingly. I make ones in stained-glass window colors (rich blue, red, turquoise, and purple) with glass "jewels" stuck on and they give a lovely gleaming quality to the light.

Toys and teddies

Do people really buy teddies for babies? Or do they buy them for themselves? My little boy has never been a big one for soft toys and everyone knows this, yet he still gets his fair share of bunnies and bears come Christmas and birthday. Whether your baby has a "fluffy" personality or not, personally I think every small person needs at least one bear—a proper bear too, with a long snout and big paws and bright glinty eyes. Such a bear is more than a toy, it's an embodiment of the great Bear spirit, one of the four wise guardians of the Native American tradition, and a powerful protective figure for your child's nursery. I carried this idea a bit further (some might say too far) when James was born. In each corner of his crib he had a guardian beanie baby: a bear, a bison (for Buffalo), a dog (for Coyote), and a rather odd-looking bird (with apologies to Eagle). Once he started being able to shunt around his crib I

moved them to a beady perch over the mantelpiece.

Make sure soft toys are suitable for the age of your baby. Read the small print on the labels as some (stupid though this may seem) are not suitable for babies younger than three years old because they have bits (eyes etc.) that can be bitten off. The bear I chose for James was a small bear made of the softest furry fleecy fabric with embroidered features. Small is good because he could easily fit in a travel-bag and the embroidered features meant he was totally safe. As is the way of the world, James rejected him in favor of a huge donkey which now has to accompany us whenever we sleep over anywhere. But do try for small—you might be luckier.

Toys don't need to be elaborate—it's a common mistake that parents make, buying toys that are too old for their baby. The second mistake is to buy too many toys. The third mistake is to buy too many toys which do all the work for the child (i.e. those all-singing, dancing electronic gizmos). These strip a child's imagination. Bricks are great. Things that surprise are good fun: Jack in the boxes, figures who jump out when the baby presses a button or pulls a lever. Toys that can be explored are wonderful—James absolutely loved the Whoozit (or spider as we called it): a soft, circular piece of fabric with lots of different textured legs and lots of hidden places for little fingers to poke and probe. Different textures invite exploration so let your baby experiment by feeling different things—not just toys but fabrics and surfaces, such as grass, sand, and water.

Spirit of Nature

Nowadays virtually everything you buy for your baby will be constructed from man-made substances—particularly plastic. It's easy to see why: plastic is hygienic, cheap, comes in bright colors, and can be molded easily into a thousand and one shapes. But does it nurture a baby's soul? I'm no purist and you'll find plenty of plastic in my house but I also think it's important to introduce our children to the natural world—and what better place to start than in the nursery?

Hopefully you will already have chosen natural wood for your furniture and pure cotton or wool for your furnishings. In this chapter we're going to look a little deeper into how to introduce the spirit of nature into your baby's cocoon.

The elements

Think about the four elements as you design your nursery. Wood is a natural for furniture but think about how you can include the other elements too:

- Large pebbles and stones (too big for a baby to swallow) are wonderful for a baby to explore, and look lovely too. A small cairn in a corner of the baby's room is grounding, as well as looking and feeling good.
- Crystals are a wonderful way to introduce Earth.
- Pieces of driftwood are sculptural and again, fascinating for little fingers. Remember that babies will try to put everything in their mouths so sterilize any outdoor finds in Milton or similar before putting them in the nursery and, again, make sure they are too big to swallow and that bits won't break off.
- We have fresh flowers all over the house but often not in the nursery. Why ever not? Choose nursery flowers for their bright colors, gorgeous scents, and interesting shapes. Make sure they are out of reach—or they could become lunch.
- Think also about little posies of wild flowers—or vases filled with branches in bud or blossom (catkins are sublime). Or simply branches of interestingly shaped leaves.
- We've already talked about water features and fountains (ensure they are out of reach) but, if that isn't possible, have a bowl of water in your nursery. Choose a beautiful bowl and fill it with fresh water every day. You might want to float petals on it.
- Babies find fire fascinating and a candle (safely positioned) is a wonderful way to bring fire energy to your nursery (few of us now have the luxury of an open fire in the nursery and, even if we did, it isn't a good idea as woodsmoke can hurt small lungs). A really safe option is to float water candles in your bowl.
- Plants can become a jungle or a forest for babies—they will be

fascinated if you bring in your cheeseplant for a daily outing and let it wave its fronds over the crib. Take it out during the night though.

- Air is a tricky one as the traditional ways of introducing it are through incense and aromatherapy oils which have to be used with great care (see Scent chapter). However, you can and should throw open the windows every day to let in the fresh air.

 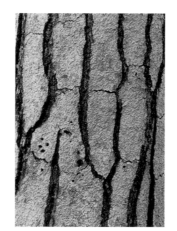 

Tree wisdom

Tree lore is fascinating. We've already talked a little about it with regard to cribs, but here are some more ideas. Oak supposedly has the power to give strength to growing children. Jacqueline Memory Paterson, author of *Tree Wisdom* (Thorsons), recounts that at the Spring Equinox people would call upon the oak to encourage the sun to shine brightly and warmly for the healthy growth of their young children. Acorns were considered magical fruit, with powers to give protection, luck, and a healthy life. You could maybe gather acorns and plant them in little pots. The strongest seedling could then be dedicated to your baby and planted as his or her own tree.

Added protection comes from rowan which was thought of by the ancients as the Tree of Life. It is said to guard the

integrity of the home and, if you can, it's lovely to have a rowan watching over your house. We don't take any chances and have several around our abode. Rowan is said also to lift the emotions and to allow relaxation—you could say it's the original stress-buster. A Rowan Cross is made of two twigs of rowan tied into a cross with red ribbon. Originally it was carried at Hallowe'en for protection against evil spirits but nowadays it is used for protection at any time and makes a lovely addition to a nursery.

Pine is another protective tree—and for many people will be the easiest wood to introduce into the nursery. Try to avoid the brashly varnished pine that seems to be everywhere and look out for old pine which is a lovely soft color (and not packed with nasty chemical varnishes).

Plants and herbs

Plants and herbs have specific magical properties too, and could be used in a nursery in various ways.

- Basil is said to protect from fears—it's an easy herb to grow so add to window boxes or plant in pots and keep on the window-ledge.
- Catnip is a wonderful children's herb: herbalists use it to soothe colic, stabilize upset stomachs, and calm jangled nerves. It's considered a friendship and love totem, drawing love, beauty, and joy to the house. Again, it's a simple herb to grow so add to your window box or put a pot on your nursery altar (see page 85).
- Lavender attracts love, joy, and a long life. It is said to open the heart, clear the mind, and bestow loving blessings. It's another one for your window box but also use dried lavender in bags to scent your nursery drawers —or put a bowl of dried lavender in your nursery.

Animal totems

Animal images and nurseries go hand in glove—when you look a little deeper at the symbolism, it's easy to see why. Particular animals have always been imagined to have particular qualities and powers. If you like this idea, you could unearth soft toys of the animals you like or find pictures of them or paint them on walls or furniture. Folkloric or native images work well. However, as babies get older they also like "real" pictures of animals and can swiftly become adept in recognizing different species of bird or various breeds of dog, for example.

Here are a few correspondences to get you started:

- Wren: A tiny bird which is a symbol of luck and love of home. It also signifies pregnancy. Often used as a charm.
- Swallow: Ushers in joy, freedom, and playfulness. It could be lovely to have swallows swooping around your walls —or on strings from the ceiling.
- Stork: The archetypal symbol of fertility, birth, courtship, and home building. Sadly most people find it a bit too hackneyed nowadays yet the stork is a beautiful bird.
- Fox: A good totem for children as they get older. The fox (and coyote) helps you make smart decisions and adapt to difficult situations. The fox is also a great believer in sheer good fun.
- Bear: As we've already discussed, bears are protective figures and so ideal for nurseries.
- Dolphin: You may be surprised to hear that dolphins are also considered archetypal "good" mothers and are therefore protective.
- Dog: Dogs are also considered protectors. They are sociable, faithful, and possess endurance. A big dog can be very comforting to a small child.

Crystals

I think it's a lovely idea to have a crystal dedicated for your child's bedroom. For many years before I had my baby, I had a large piece of polished rose quartz which I adored. When we were sorting out James' nursery I had a sudden compelling feeling that this was actually "his" crystal. So it was duly cleansed and dedicated and has sat in his room ever since, keeping a loving and slightly beady eye on him.

Rose quartz is a good safe choice for babies and young children—it is a warm and protective stone, very gentle and loving. Rose quartz is connected with the heart chakra and is associated with unconditional love, peace, comfort, and reassurance. It is also often used in crystal healing for soothing sleeplessness. Do you need any more reasons to have one in your nursery?

However, rose quartz is not the only choice—here are some other crystals to consider:

- **Pink agate**: Said to promote love between parent and child. It's a soothing, grounding stone.
- **Coral**: Traditionally considered good for children, it provides safety and wards off danger and fear.
- **Carnelian**: Useful if your baby had a rocky start to life (maybe premature or sickly). It has the power to anchor babies in the physical world, as it is strongly linked to the Earth. It is also said to align you with your life's purpose, which might sound strange for a baby—but many say we bring our life's purpose with us from birth.
- **Amber**: A useful stone if you feel your baby or child needs protection from negative energy. It is also a good

choice if you live in a polluted area as it is said to help clear toxins.

- **Emerald**: A lovely stone which harmonizes heart energy and is said to bestow joy and vitality.
- **Topaz**: Another life-affirming, joyful stone which gives energy and warmth. It opens up possibilities and can usher in abundance.
- **Hermatite**: A stone which was believed to confer invincibility on the owner— it's certainly very protective. It also fosters self-worth and confidence— vital gifts for a child.
- **Tiger's Eye**: Said to draw helpful people to the owner, it also is traditionally associated with abundance and wealth (but in a natural, balanced way).
- **Chalcedony**: Useful for older babies and toddlers who may suffer from night terrors, bad dreams, and nightmares. It also counteracts fear of the dark. This stone is said to drive away nightmares and ease fear.

You may also want to let your intuition guide you. Go into a crystal shop and browse around until a stone or stones "calls" to you. It may sound silly but, trust me, you will find some stones are almost irresistible. Just check that you're focusing on your wishes for your baby, rather than yourself.

Spirit of Blessing

By now you should have come to realize that a nursery is far more than just a physical entity: it is a sacred space. This chapter helps you consecrate and bless your nursery.

Consecrating your nursery is a lovely ceremony—it offers your baby a psychic welcome to your home (even if he or she is yet to be born). Before you perform this ritual you will need to have thoroughly space cleansed your nursery (remember, if you are pregnant, ask someone to do it for you—maybe your partner, your child's prospective godparent, or a grandparent).

See page 11 for how to space cleanse. However, this ritual is something you *can* do, even if you are pregnant.

Nursery consecration

Choose a time to perform this ritual when you are feeling calm, confident, and full of joy. Your mood is very important so don't do it if you're feeling at all tense, tired, or irritable. You will need a pink or gold candle, some lavender essential oil, a bowl of warm water, and four pretty pebbles or crystals.

1 Sit yourself in the center of the room, light your candle, and spend some time just sitting and being. Pay attention to your breathing—don't try to change it, just notice how it gradually slows down and deepens.

2 If you have a guardian angel or a power animal or any connections with particular spiritual beings, you might want to ask them for their help and guidance in this. Send up a quiet prayer to them.

3 Let five drops of lavender oil fall into the bowl of water—watch the rainbow oil spread and inhale the delicious scent. As each drop hits the water imagine it is sending out a spark of loving energy into each corner of the room. The last drop goes to the middle and then you imagine all five joining together.

4 Start to breathe into your heart center and imagine that within you is a swirling vortex of beautiful pink-gold light. It bubbles up within you and then bursts out into the room, suffusing it with a gentle golden glow.

5 Gradually you have a sense of four great guardians standing, one in each corner. These are the four great Archangels:

- Raphael is the archangel of the east, he comes clothed in amber and gold.

- Gabriel guards the west; he is clad in robes of violet and silver, shining like the moon.

- Michael is archangel of the south, who wears a glowing orange cloak over his glittering gold armor.

- Uriel protects the north, his robes are black and yellow.

6 Ask these great figures to guard and protect your baby. You may have a sense that they agree. Give them grateful thanks.

7 Now hold the pebbles or crystals in your hand and imagine the pink-gold light of your heart is infusing them too. Place one in each corner of the room to remind you of the angels' presence. (Note: remove them once your baby starts crawling and exploring—they are just too tempting and will end up in small mouths).

8 Softly blow out your candle. Leave your bowl of water where it is for a while.

Although I use the archangels in this blessing, it is not specifically a Christian ceremony. The idea of archangels or mighty spirits occurs in many religions. This one is loosely based on Qabalistic principles but you could substitute your own choice of guardians if this does not resonate with you.

Making a nursery altar

A nursery altar is a lovely way of focusing your hopes and wishes for your baby. It's something you can start well before your baby is born, when it can be used as a focus for your own meditation and musings. Once the baby arrives you may find you want to make changes to reflect your baby's personality.

There's nothing spooky about having an altar in your baby's room. It's simply a place of spiritual focus; somewhere that makes you mindful of the world beyond dirty nappies and sleepless nights. If you're religious you can add sacred elements from your faith. If not, you can be more free-form. There really are no set rules for altar-building—it's a chance to be as creative as you like. If you feel uncertain, however, there are various tried and tested formulae which will start you on the right track.

Traditionally you would place an altar on a table top or on a special low table—but there are many other sites. How about on a mantelpiece, a shelf, or a window ledge? Alternatively, if you are short on space, you could buy a hanging basket (or one of the three or four-tiered series of baskets) and suspend it from a hook in the ceiling.

Having picked your spot, cover it with an altar cloth. This is basically a piece of fabric which marks out your space. It might be traditional linen or you could be more inventive. Think about the following: a fleece baby blanket, an appliquéd cover, an embroidered cloth (with suitable motifs), a sheepskin, a wool checked blanket, a so-soft pashmina, a glittering sari, a tribal weaving...

Next you add items which represent the elements—for balance. Traditionally these would be:

- A bowl of water (choose a beautiful bowl—maybe something hand-made or a pretty china dish). You might like to add pebbles from the ocean or river, or float petals or flowers on the water.
- A candle to represent Fire. Pink is the classic color for babyhood (it's very protective), but green is very balancing. Again, choose a pretty candlestick or holder.
- Something to represent Earth. This could be a small pot of salt or perhaps a beautiful stone or something made of clay.
- An incense or aromatherapy burner to represent Air. Remember, once your baby is in residence, you will have to be very careful with burning anything pungent.

Now add items to personalize your altar. You might like to include some of the following:

- A photo of your baby (or perhaps a scan picture).
- Photos of people who will be or are important for your baby (yourselves as

parents; grandparents, godparents, or siblings).

- If you have a favorite deity it is good to include an image or symbol: a figure of Buddha or the Goddess; a cross or Star of David.
- Might your baby have a guardian? Think about images or figures of guardian angels or power animals.
- The Romans had deities for absolutely everything: Alemona is the Roman goddess of fetuses; Cuba is the Roman goddess of children's sleep (well worth invoking); her sister Cunina protects infants in their cradles. You could also track down other guardians from different cultures.
- Crystals are lovely healers—look at the ideas on page 79.
- Beloved toys or books from your own childhood—or your own christening gifts.

- A special teddy bear or small items you have bought for the baby.
- Little cards with your hopes and prayers for your baby—you might like to pick out some of the Angel cards or make your own with words like "Love," or "Joy" on them. Perhaps everyone who comes to your house could inscribe their own blessings for the baby and add them to the altar.
- A little pot of flowers (simple spring bulbs maybe, or daisies, or sweet peas).

Runes

Runes are an ancient sacred alphabet which are often used in divination. However, you can also use them as protective symbols for your nursery. Traditionally one would carve them into wood (rowan, oak, or elder would be ideal) or paint them onto pebbles. You could also

carve them into the wood of your baby's crib or into a piece of wood to be hung from the door or wall. Here are the runes which would be most appropriate for a nursery with some of their meanings.

Thorn for protection
Wynn for happiness, harmony, and joy
Jara for healing and vital energy
Beorc for new beginnings and to invoke the Goddess
Ur for strength and courage
Feoh for abundance and prosperity

Endings and beginnings

We've come to the end of this little book now and I hope it has given you pleasure and inspiration. Now all that remains is to wish you and your baby limitless joy, deep peace, wonderful nights of deep restorative sleep (no harm in wishing), and above all fun, fun, fun.

Resources

All the flower essences and room sprays mentioned can be obtained from The International Flower Essence Repertoire. **flower@atlas.co.uk or +44 (0) 20 1428 741572**

The Healthy House is a great company that offers all manner of products for the home—from allergy-free bedding to monitors to check magnetic radiation. **www.healthy-house.co.uk or +44 (0) 20 1453 752216**

Natural Mat stocks natural fiber crib and crib mattresses, unbleached sheets, blankets, fleeces etc. **www.naturalmat.com or +44 (0) 20 20 7689 0990**

www.urchin.co.uk is a great place to find quirky nursery gear. They also stock several of the things mentioned in this book: i.e. good mobiles, sheepskin rugs, the bedside crib, animal rugs, groovy storage, paint-on lanterns, sleeping bags, Whoozits, even organic comfort toys! They'll ship all over the world.

www.keepbabysafe.net is a useful website with valuable information on babyproofing.

If you're looking for something a bit more avant-garde than the standard nursery furniture check out **www.orekakids.com**

Precious Earth is a good source for environmentally friendly and eco-sensitive solutions to decorating needs. **www.preciousearth.co.uk**

Books

There aren't really any good books on nurseries, which was why I wanted to write this one. However, there are plenty of wonderful books which have inspired me—I'm listing some here in the hope they might do the same for you.

- *Nursery.* This was the little book which initially inspired me. I loved its design but wanted more information on the nursery itself—but it's still a great book.
- *Mother and Child* by Jan Reynolds. Not a book about nurseries but about parenting in indigenous cultures. The photographs are fabulous and offer inspiration at a tangent.
- *Aromatherapy for your Child* by Valerie Ann Worwood. Highly useful as your baby gets older.

- *The Incarnating Child* by Joan Salter. A magical book with fascinating insights into the spiritual development of babies and children.
- *Caretaking a New Soul* by Anne Carson. A collection of eye-opening spiritual writings on parenting.
- *Parenting for a Healthy Future* by Dotty Coplen. An excellent guide for parents with emphasis on spiritual and psychological growth.
- *The What to Expect series* by Arlene Eisenberg, Heidi E Murkoff and Sandee E Hathaway. These invaluable, practical, and down-to-earth guides on everything you could want to know about pregnancy, babies, and toddlers have been my bibles.

Picture Credits